WHO LIVES
IN THE
WOODS?

Illustrated by Rudolf Freund

Adapted from the original text by Dena Humphreys

Copyright © 1987, 1979, 1951 by Grosset & Dunlap, a member of
The Putnam Publishing Group, New York. All rights reserved.
Published simultaneously in Canada. Printed in Singapore.
ISBN 0-448-46537-X A B C D E F G H I J
Previously published as *The Big Book of Animals Every Child
Should Know*, also as *Animals Every Child Should Know.*

Platt & Munk, Publishers • New York

A division of Grosset & Dunlap

GRAY SQUIRREL

The gray squirrel has a long, fluffy tail. It looks extremely handsome and helps to balance him. He can sit on the branch of a tall tree and never worry about falling off. Besides, he has long-fingered paws. It is easy for him to leap and scurry through the treetops, where he has built a secret nest made of twigs and leaves.

When the squirrel is on the ground he hunts for nuts and acorns. These are the squirrel's favorite foods. But he never stuffs himself too full of them. He eats only as many as he needs. He hides the rest down under rocks and leaves. Sometimes he digs a hole and buries them. Then, on some wintry day when food is hard to find, he will dig up the acorns and have a feast.

CHIPMUNK

Sometimes the chipmunk's head looks wider than his body. That is because his cheeks are stuffed full of nuts. The chipmunk is collecting food for the long winter ahead.

All summer long the chipmunk works so he can rest in the winter. He digs himself a cozy hole under a tree or maybe deep among some rocks. In his hole he stores nuts and acorns, berries, seeds, and grain. When the cold weather comes he goes to sleep down at the bottom of his hole. Once in a while he wakes, uncurls himself, and has a bite to eat. But mostly he just sleeps.

Though the chipmunk is small, he is quick and brave. He always wants to know what is going on. If someone puts peanuts in the grass, he will eat the first one that he finds. He holds it daintily in his tiny paws and nibbles fast. Then he tucks the rest of the peanuts into his cheeks to carry home.

RED FOX

The red fox is not really red like a tomato. He is a bright, reddish orange-brown all tipped in black. He may have a dash of white trimming too. His ears are often black. So are his slender paws, his thin, sharp nose, and sometimes even his long, bushy tail.

The fox is just a little larger than a cat, but he makes up for his small size by being smart and quick. He is also sly and full of tricks. That is what "foxy" means.

The fox's home is a secret cave dug in a bank of earth. There the fox cubs huddle cozily while the father and mother go hunting. When mother fox takes the cubs out to frisk in the sun, she shows them where to catch frogs and fish and other little creatures for food. Foxes like to eat fruit, too.

There are many kinds of foxes, and they can be different colors. But foxes are rarely seen. That is because they are clever and stay hidden.

PORCUPINE

The porcupine is not fierce or strong or quick so he needs his sharp quills to keep harmful creatures away. He cannot shoot the quills out of his skin. When he is frightened or angry, he shakes himself. Then loose quills scatter all around. New quills will grow out to take the place of the quills that were shed. The quills have tiny hooks along the ends to make them stick into things. Of course those quills hurt, and no one ever tries to pat a porcupine.

The porcupine has claws that are curved. This helps him to climb trees. He uses his sharp front teeth to rip off the outside bark of branches and twigs. Then he nibbles the green juicy parts underneath.

Porcupines usually mind their own business. But sometimes they wander into empty cabins and poke around until they find something to gnaw on—the handle of a wooden spoon or sharp ax, for instance.

OPOSSUM

The possum's real name is opossum, but hardly anyone calls him that. When the possum doesn't want to be noticed, he pretends to be asleep. If any enemy approaches him, he curls up in a ball and stays quite still until the intruder goes away. The possum is only the size of a cat, and he cannot run very fast. He is not fierce. So the best thing for him to do when he suspects danger is near is to "play possum."

Possums have short, thick fur, but long hairs are scattered all over them besides. Their bare, gray tails help them to climb trees, curling around the branches like an extra hand. They can even hang upside down by their tails. Their hind paws are like hands, too, because they have thumbs for holding onto things.

When the mother possum goes looking for grasshoppers, grubs, beetles, and fruit, she takes her babies with her. The babies cling to her back as she lumbers along.

RABBITS

Rabbits are soft. They have large, gentle eyes and wiggly noses and small, white tails that look like powder puffs. Some people call them "cottontails."

Wild rabbits live in secret homes along the edges of the woods. They dig small holes in the earth to keep their babies warm and safe while they are small. Their noses seem to twitch all the time to sniff out trouble. Their eyes are watchful. Their long ears turn to catch sounds of danger. If something startles them, they scamper under a low-growing shrub. A rabbit's fur is grayish brown, the color of dead leaves and old dry grasses. So when a rabbit lies very still it is scarcely noticed at all.

WOODCHUCK

In autumn, when the air grows chilly, the woodchuck begins to feel quite lazy. By and by, he feels so drowsy that he crawls into his home, a hole dug deep down in the ground. There he curls up and falls asleep. While the woodchuck sleeps, his body does not stay warm and cozy. It cools off fast. But thick fur and a nice layer of fat under the woodchuck's skin keep him from freezing through and through.

Near springtime the woodchuck wakes up from his long winter sleep. When he goes outside at the beginning of February, people say it is "Groundhog Day." Groundhog is another name for the woodchuck.

The woodchuck wakes up very thin. He starts eating right away to get fat. It is not hard because he eats so many different things—roots and twigs, buds and grasses, nuts and seeds, berries and other fruit, and insects. By the time the cold weather arrives again, the woodchuck is so fat he waddles just a little as he walks.

WHITE-FOOTED FIELD MOUSE

Sometimes the field mouse eats strange things— candles and soap, for instance. Of course, the field mouse doesn't find candles and soap in the woods and fields where he is supposed to live. But mice are bold, even though they are quite small. They come right into people's houses and make themselves at home. They like barns, too, especially where there is warm hay and lots of seed and grain.

The field mouse has a sleek coat with white fur down the front. His eyes and ears are large, and he has quivery whiskers. Inside a house he gnaws and chews all kinds of things. His nibbling probably damages more food than he eats.

Some people say "quiet as a mouse." But unless a mouse is frightened, he is not so very quiet. In old country houses mice often squeak and scamper about all night long.

OTTER

The otter looks cheerful. He likes to play. He loves to slide down waterfalls. He even teases other otters to play with him.

When the otter is tired he scrambles up onto the shore. His paddle feet make a moist, squishy noise. On his head the pale underfur shows through and makes his face seem frosty.

Otters live in the faraway wild woods, by lakes and streams. They make hidden nests for their babies. They line their homes with soft, dry grass and leaves. And they are so shy that people seldom see them. But in zoos otters grow tame. At feeding time they run at the keeper's heels like big, eager dogs. To run they have to arch their backs because their legs are so short and their bodies are so long.

Otters are full of fun, even the old ones. They seem never to grow up.

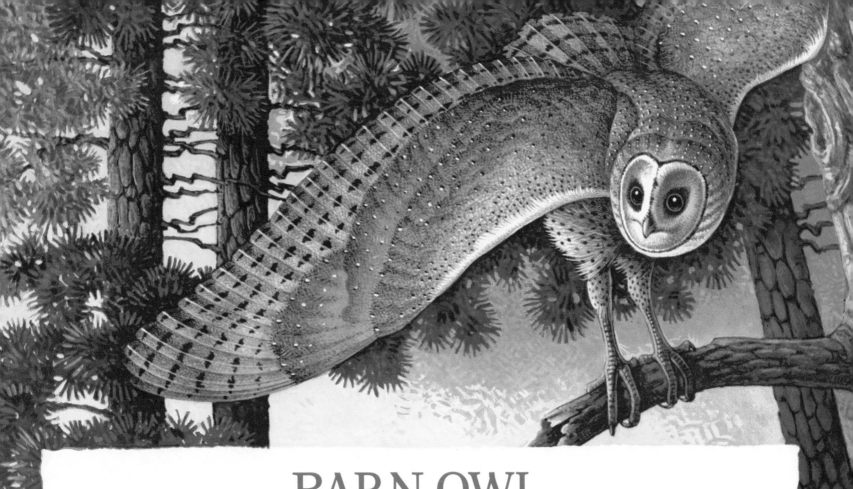

BARN OWL

Barn owls live near farms. By day the barn owl likes to stay hidden in a hollow tree or some snug hole among the rocks. He sleeps or else keeps his eyes almost closed because of the bright sunshine. When night comes, he hunts for mice and fish and even snakes. He swoops down through the dim forest on soft, silent wings. He can see well by starlight.

The owl has a flat face, a round head, and a neck that does not show because his feathers cover it. His eyes do not move. To look at things the owl has to turn his head until it seems to be on backward.

Most owls are brown or gray, with handsome stripes. Some owls have tufts of feathers on their heads shaped like a cat's ears or like tiny horns. Sometimes owls call "Whoo-hoo-hoo-hooo" from the dark forest.

Unless he is hunting, the owl seldom moves. Even a young owl can sit so still and stare so hard that people like to call him "wise old owl."

SKUNK

Skunks do not mind the smell of skunk. All other creatures do. Often in the country on summer nights there comes a whiff of something odd and sharp in the air, the strangest smell ever. That means that somewhere a skunk has felt annoyed.

Skunks can give off this smell whenever they want to. They never need to run or fight. Skunks are naturally peaceful and bother nobody unless they are bothered first.

The skunk never has to hide, so his coloring does not match woodsy things like rocks and trees. He has a gorgeous

black coat of long, thick fur with two white stripes down the back.

Baby skunks can't spray a scent until they are quite grown up. They stay close to their mother when she prowls through the woods and fields, searching for food. The babies' small striped backs bob along behind the mother's big one, and all their fluffy white-tipped tails gaily stand straight up in the air.

RACCOON

The raccoon looks much bigger than he is, because of his thick, deep fur. It stands up as straight as long grass in a field. He has black rings around his tail, and the black pattern on his face makes him look surprised and puzzled all the time.

The raccoon's paws aren't made for walking only. He has thin curling fingers to help him climb trees. When twilight comes he scrambles down and prowls for food. He will eat almost anything—nuts and berries, minnows and crabs, and much more besides.

The raccoon likes his meals to be very soft and wet. He carries his food to a stream and dips it in the water. Then he rubs and kneads it with his paws before he eats.

Raccoons live where there are lots of trees and not too many people.

BEAVER

The beaver is a sticky-looking creature. That is because he is usually wet. Even when it is cold he swims and swims. The beaver can swim fast making no splash or sound. Then sometimes he lies so still that he could be mistaken for a floating log. If he hears someone coming he slaps the water hard with his tail. It is wide and flat just like a leather paddle. The noise it makes hitting the top of the water warns his friends of danger.

Beavers have two big, sharp front teeth. Beavers use their front teeth like chisels to chop down trees. They eat the bark and twigs and leaves. They use the branches to build houses and dams.

Beavers build their houses in northern woods wherever there are lakes and streams. The house is a round island made of mud and branches. Inside the house beavers build a nice dry shelf to sleep on. Beaver babies live in the house while they are small. They are safe because the door is under water. No enemy creature can get inside.

The beaver always seems to be cutting down trees, even when he does not need them. No wonder people talk of being "busy as a beaver."